AWAKEN MORE ZEAL

A STUDY GUIDE FOR

ZEALOUS
7 COMMITMENTS FOR
THE DISCIPLESHIP OF
THE NEXT GENERATIONS

DAVID MICHAEL
SHERRI MORAN

Truth:78

Awaken More Zeal: A Study Guide for Zealous: 7 Commitments for the Discipleship of the Next Generations

By Sherri Moran based on content in *Zealous: 7 Commitments for the Discipleship of the Next Generations* by David Michael

Our vision at Truth78 is that the next generations know, honor, and treasure God, setting their hope in Christ alone, so that they will live as faithful disciples for the glory of God. Our mission is to inspire and equip the church and the home for the comprehensive discipleship of the next generation.

We equip churches and parents by producing curriculum for Sunday School, Midweek, Multi-Age, Youth, and Backyard Bible Club settings; vision-casting and training resources (many available free on our website) for both the church and the home; materials and training to help parents in their role in discipling children; and the Fighter Verses™ Bible memory program to encourage the lifelong practice and love of Bible memory.

Published in the United States of America by Truth78.

ISBN: 978-1-952783-94-4

Equipping the Next Generations to Know, Honor, and Treasure God

Truth78.org
info@Truth78.org
(877) 400-1414

To all who are striving side by side with us for the faith of the gospel, may you be encouraged to press on in zeal, by God's grace, for the everlasting joy of the next generation.

Give ear, O my people, to my teaching;
    incline your ears to the words of my mouth!
I will open my mouth in a parable;
    I will utter dark sayings from of old,
things that we have heard and known,
    that our fathers have told us.
We will not hide them from their children,
    but tell to the coming generation
the glorious deeds of the LORD, and his might,
    and the wonders that he has done.

He established a testimony in Jacob
    and appointed a law in Israel,
which he commanded our fathers
    to teach to their children,
that the next generation might know them,
    the children yet unborn,
and arise and tell them to their children,
    so that they should set their hope in God
and not forget the works of God,
    but keep his commandments;
and that they should not be like their fathers,
    a stubborn and rebellious generation,
a generation whose heart was not steadfast,
    whose spirit was not faithful to God.

PSALM 78:1-8

Contents

Introduction

This study guide is a companion to *Zealous: 7 Commitments for the Discipleship of the Next Generations.* You can order print copies, download complimentary digital copies of the book or audiobook, and see additional resources at Truth78.org/Zealous.

As you consider the biblical vision and framework you have in place (or seek to establish) for discipling the children and youth in your church or home, may God give you all the grace you need to embrace, prioritize, and faithfully fulfill the responsib ility we share as God's people to "tell to the coming generation the glorious deeds of the LORD, and his might, and the wonders that he has done" (Psalm 78:4).

HOW TO USE THIS GUIDE

Our intention is to create a space for you to further explore the content of *Zealous* individually and with your ministry team, spouse, fellow parents, or other groups. Each section includes the following:

- **Key Scriptures**—some of the Bible verses referenced in *Zealous* to re-read and consider studying further
- **Reflection**—insights and prompts to help you prayerfully process the main ideas from each chapter of *Zealous*
- **Discussion**—questions for your group to use to evaluate your discipleship efforts in your churches and homes
- **Next Steps**—ideas for more application, activities, and recommended resources

For God's glory and the everlasting joy of all generations (Ephesians 3:21) in all nations (Matthew 28:19),

The Truth78 Team

Zeal that Matters

From Genesis to Revelation, everything we are called to do in the service of our King, including the discipleship of the next generation, requires zeal... Zeal in Scripture is not simply enthusiasm. It is fervor and diligence born out of a passion for God and His glory. It is the result of a heart on fire for the glory of God that is uncontainable and spills out in zealous evangelism, discipleship, service, and good works. (Zealous, page 13)

KEY SCRIPTURES

"You shall love the LORD your God with all your heart and with all your soul and with all your might. And these words that I command you today shall be on your heart. You shall teach them diligently to your children, and shall talk of them when you sit in your house, and when you walk by the way, and when you lie down, and when you rise." (Deuteronomy 6:5-7)

Him we proclaim, warning everyone and teaching everyone with all wisdom, that we may present everyone mature in Christ. For this I toil, struggling with all his energy that he powerfully works within me. (Colossians 1:28-29)

Brothers, my heart's desire and prayer to God for them is that they may be saved. For I bear them witness that they have a zeal for God, but not according to knowledge. (Romans 10:1-2)

REFLECTION

Our hearts are passionate about many things, but are they the right things—the things that matter? When we as pastors, ministry leaders, parents, grandparents, and others are zealous for discipleship, it can make a significant difference in the lives of the children growing up in our churches and homes. Sometimes it's hard to know where to start and what zealous discipleship looks like in everyday life. The first step toward awakening zeal (fervor, diligence, passion) for the things that matter to God is to acknowledge our inability to make ourselves zealous. We can ask God to ignite zeal in our hearts so that we labor with energy that comes from Him—energy born out of a desire for His glory. Zeal is a good gift from God that motivates and sustains our efforts. This kind of zeal is different from enthusiasm for other pursuits. It is also contagious and may be just what God uses to inspire others.

Take time to reflect on why zeal for the discipleship of children and youth matters to God and how He uses it to accomplish His sovereign purposes. Is zeal currently expressed in your family or ministry? If so, how is it currently shown? If not, God is eager to help His children. Ask God to ignite (or re-ignite) zeal in your own heart that is uncontainable and overflows to inspire others, for His glory.

DISCUSSION

1. What are some concerns (or deep "wonderings") that you have about the spiritual state of the children in your life, church, or elsewhere? How do these concerns point to the need for individual and collective biblical motivation?

2. How does zeal for God connect to the discipleship of children in Deuteronomy 6:5-7? What other Scriptures come to mind, perhaps from this chapter in *Zealous*?

3. What is the difference between laboring in your own strength and "struggling with all his energy that he powerfully works within [you]"? When you look at your ministry labors, do they seem fueled by self-effort or dependency on God? What can you do to lean on God's strength more? (See Colossians 1:28-29.)

4. Discuss the difference between zeal for God (and godly things) that is according to knowledge versus zeal that is not according to knowledge (Romans 10:1-4).

On a scale of 1-10, how would you rate the level of zeal for the next generation in your church or your family overall?

Lacking Zeal 1 2 3 4 5 6 7 8 9 10 Bursting with Zeal

What is one thing that you or your ministry team could commit to that would grow this number?

NEXT STEPS

Ministry leaders—List the various programs, activities, and events that promote the discipleship of the next generation in your church or ministry. What purpose are they serving? Rank them according to priority and potential spiritual impact. Evaluate their effectiveness.

Parents—What activities contribute to the discipleship of your children? Are you satisfied with the amount of time being invested in their discipleship versus other pursuits? What steps can you take to prioritize and improve upon your efforts to disciple your children?

Ministry leaders and parents—Review the following aspects of zeal and corresponding Scriptures. What steps can you take in your ministry or parenting to grow, with the energy God provides (*Zealous*, pages 17-19)?

- Zeal according to knowledge (Romans 10:1-4)
- Zeal for our children's children's children (Psalm 78:5-7)
- Zeal for strong faith in a world of hostility (Luke 21:17; John 15:19)
- Zeal for duty and delight (Hebrews 12:2-3; John 1:4; Psalm 16:11)

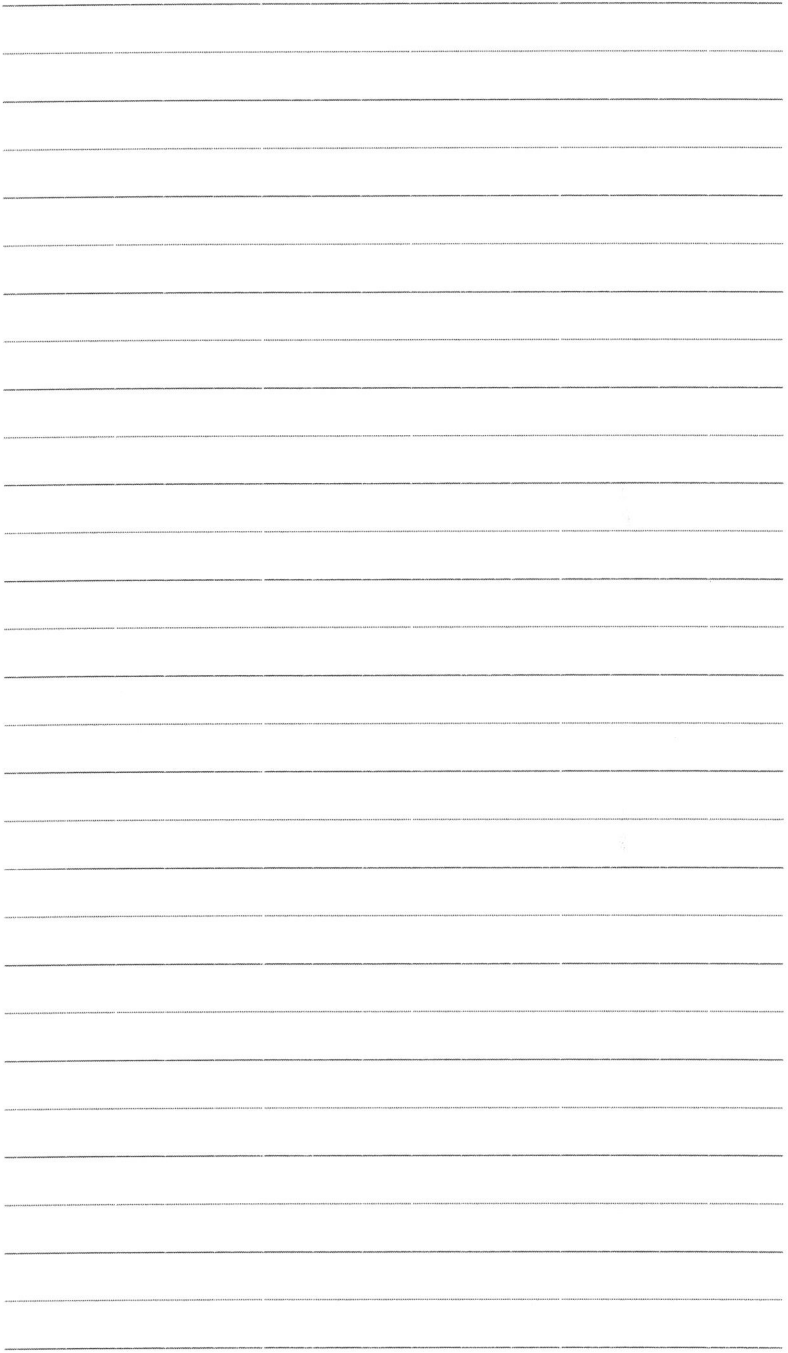

AWAKEN MORE ZEAL WITH 7 COMMITMENTS

1 ▾ Embrace a Biblical Vision for the Faith of the Next Generation

2 ▾ Foster a Robust Partnership Between Church and Home

3 ▾ Teach the Breadth and Depth of the Whole Counsel of God

4 ▾ Proclaim the Glorious Gospel of Jesus Christ

5 ▾ Disciple the Mind, Heart, and Will

6 ▾ Pray with Dependence on God's Sovereign Grace

7 ▾ Inspire Worship of God, for the Glory of God

1

Embrace a Biblical Vision for the Faith of the Next Generation

An activity-oriented ministry puts more emphasis on the present, and less, if any at all, on the future. [Activity-oriented programs] concentrate more on what they are doing with the children, and less on where they are leading the children…A vision-oriented program or activity is clearly linked to specific discipleship goals that are fueled by prayer and the desire for children to whole-heartedly embrace Christ. Vision-oriented parents, Christian educators, and church leaders think about and act according to what they want to be true of their children 10, 20, and 40 years hence. (Zealous, page 26)

KEY SCRIPTURES

*Behold, children are a heritage from the LORD,
the fruit of the womb a reward.
Like arrows in the hand of a warrior
are the children of one's youth.
Blessed is the man
who fills his quiver with them!
He shall not be put to shame
when he speaks with his enemies in the gate. (Psalm 127:3-5)*

For we are God's fellow workers. You are God's field, God's building. According to the grace of God given to me, like a skilled master builder I laid a foundation, and someone else is building upon it. Let each one take care how he builds upon it. For no one can lay a foundation other than that which is laid, which is Jesus Christ. (1 Corinthians 3:9-11)

REFLECTION

Leading with vision means that our deepest desires are centered on the everlasting joy of our children and focused on the care and concern for their souls. When we embrace a biblical vision for discipleship, our aim is for the next generation to know and delight in God and His Word, treasure Christ as their eternal hope, and live with a God-centered orientation for their whole lives. This commitment sets the stage for all other commitments and serves as the overarching passion, conviction, and mindset for our efforts in the church and at home. A vision-oriented approach to discipleship helps us clarify goals and informs an intentional plan to pursue those goals. Every program, activity, curriculum, and resource can be evaluated for alignment with the greater vision we are pursuing—with zeal.

What are your dreams and desires for the children in your sphere of influence? How do they align with an overall biblical vision? Ask God for a fresh perspective and mindset to pursue a biblical vision for discipleship in whatever role or capacity He has given you.

DISCUSSION

1. What differences do you see between Pastor Program and Pastor Vision? Which approach has informed your understanding of next-generation ministry? In what ways?

2. How might a vision-oriented approach to discipleship influence the activities and priorities for children and youth in your church and family?

3. Consider the "arrows" image in Psalm 127:3-5. How would you define the target for the children and youth in your church and family?

4. What implications does 1 Corinthians 3:9-17 have for next-generation discipleship in your church or family?

5. Consider the four ways to ignite zeal described on pages 29-33. What ideas do you have for growing more zeal in these areas?

_____

_____

_____

_____

On a scale of 1-10, how would you rate your church's or family's biblical vision for the next generation overall?

No Biblical Vision 1 2 3 4 5 6 7 8 9 10 Strong Biblical Vision

What is one thing that you or your ministry team could commit to that would grow this number?

_____

_____

NEXT STEPS

Take some time to answer the questions on page 27 of *Zealous*. What do you want to be true of the children growing up in your church or home 10, 20, and 40 years from now...and beyond? Let specific verses or passages of Scripture shape your answers.

- What do we want our children to know and understand about God and His Word?
- What do we want them to understand about the gospel?
- What marks of faith and spiritual maturity do we want them to have?
- What portions of the Bible do we want them to be able to quote from memory by the time they graduate from high school?
- What kind of husband and father, or wife and mother do we want them to be?
- What do we want them to teach their children?
- How would we want them to respond when tragedy strikes or when they face suffering in their lives?
- What will fortify them against the temptations of wealth, pleasure, and success?

- What do we want them to be trusting in when they are taking their last breath?

Let your answers to these questions help shape a written, biblical vision statement for the children in your church or home.

Take steps to involve your pastors and elders in shaping, affirming, and communicating this vision for the next generation in your church. Consider how this vision will be regularly reinforced for parents, teachers, volunteers, and the church as a whole. The statement can serve as the beginning of a strategic ministry plan that integrates the 7 Commitments and other next steps as you move along in this study. For now, make sure Commitment #1 is incorporated into your plan.

TRUTH78 RESOURCES

- Foundations for Ministry (Truth78.org/foundations-for-ministry)
- *Indestructible Joy for the Next Generations* edited by David and Sally Michael

OTHER RESOURCES

- *The Christian Father's Present to His Children* by John Angell James (available free online)

Note: Resources and training materials related to each commitment are available from or recommended by Truth78. Training is available at Truth78.org/training, and resources are available at Truth78.org/products.

_____

_____

_____

_____

_____

_____

_____

_____

_____

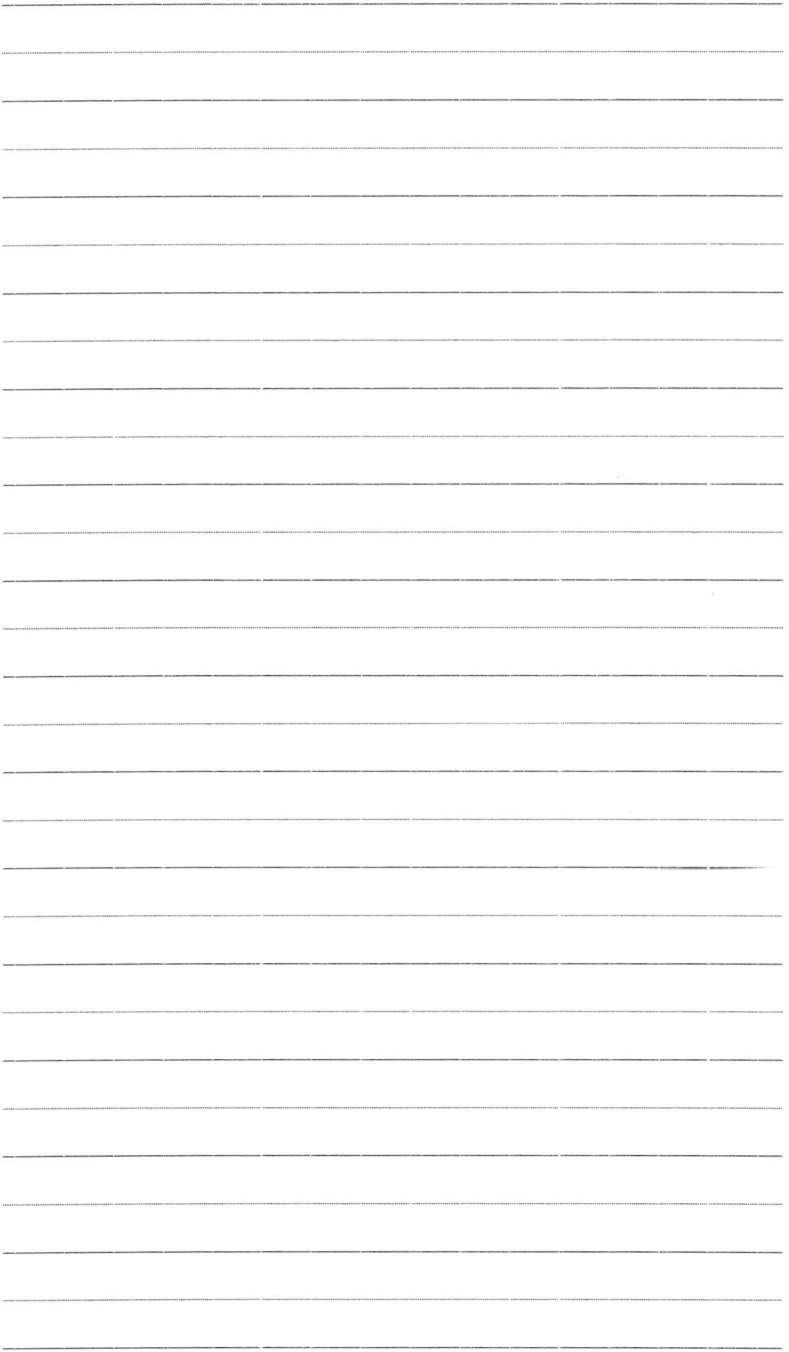

2

Foster a Robust Partnership Between Church and Home

Together, the church and home can accomplish more for the discipleship of the next generation than what could be done by either institution alone. Each brings influence and resources the other does not have. Thus, focusing on the powerful impact their partnership can have is vital. (Zealous, page 40)

KEY SCRIPTURES

Fathers, do not provoke your children to anger, but bring them up in the discipline and instruction of the Lord. (Ephesians 6:4)

And he gave the apostles, the prophets, the evangelists, the shepherds and teachers, to equip the saints for the work of ministry, for building up the body of Christ, until we all attain to the unity of the faith and of the knowledge of the Son of God, to mature manhood, to the measure of the stature of the fullness of Christ, (Ephesians 4:11-13)

*We will not hide them from their children,
but tell to the coming generation
the glorious deeds of the LORD, and his might,
and the wonders that he has done.
He established a testimony in Jacob
and appointed a law in Israel,
which he commanded our fathers
to teach to their children, (Psalm 78:4-5)*

REFLECTION

There is comfort in knowing that the biblical responsibility we bear individually for passing our faith to the next generation is not a weight we bear alone. It is a beautiful means of God's grace for local churches and homes to partner together in their discipleship efforts. The combined influences of church and home can make a powerful impact on the lives of children beyond what either institution can fully do on its own. It is a gift when parents can be a part of a church congregation that offers encouragement, training, and support. It is also a tremendous asset to the next-generation ministry in the church when parents are actively engaged in the discipleship of their children. A *robust* partnership born out of zeal with biblical vision is what God has called both the church and home to pursue together.

Are the distinct and crucial roles of the church and home clear to you and the other parents and leaders of your church? What fresh initiatives might facilitate greater understanding and forge a stronger partnership? Ask God for insights and creative ideas.

DISCUSSION

1. In what ways are the Johnson and Willis families "failing to fully see and understand an important responsibility and means of grace that God has designed for their children's discipleship" (*Zealous*, pages 35-36)?

2. Does a tension between two extremes (page 36) exist in your church or family/extended family? What might be hindering parents of either extreme from growing toward a more balanced and biblical perspective?

3. In what ways could "an effective and fruitful ministry to men" in your church (page 41) help advance your discipleship efforts at church and in your family?

4. How could your church inspire, encourage, and challenge parents to leverage their influence for the discipleship of their children?

On a scale of 1-10, rate how firmly the partnership between church and home is established in your ministry overall.

Not Established 1   2   3   4   5   6   7   8   9   10   Firmly Established

What is one thing that you or your ministry team could commit to that would grow this number?

_____

_____

NEXT STEPS

Ministry leaders—Incorporate Commitment #2 into your plan.

- Consider adding sections that communicate the biblical basis for partnership between the church and home, the church's role, the parents' role, and any details of partnership that you have in place or desire to pursue.

- What vision, instruction, training, and support do you offer parents? How do you communicate responsibility for the discipleship of the next generation beyond parents to grandparents, teachers, and the congregation as a whole? Find ways to specifically address ministry to husbands and fathers.

- Consider important milestones in life, such as child dedication, starting school, baptism, graduation, marriage, etc. How can you use those special moments to reinforce a vision for the discipleship of the next generation, emphasize your commitment to support parents, and rally the congregation to take the responsibility seriously?

Parents—Consider your present involvement in your local church and opportunities to partner with the pastors and ministry leaders who have the responsibility for ministry to children and youth.

- Are you familiar with the vision and philosophy of your church when it comes to the discipleship of the next generation?

- Is participation in worship and other aspects of church life encouraged for the whole family?

- Are there additional training opportunities that you would benefit from?

- Are there ways you can partner with the leaders of your church in serving other parents and families?

Consider these opportunities and take the next reasonable step toward growth. Don't forget that prayer is one of the most strategic investments you can make in the faith of the next generation. It's also a great way to encourage and support the leaders of your church!

TRUTH78 RESOURCES

- Partnering with Your Church (Truth78.org/partnering-with-your-church)
- Partnering with Parents (Truth78.org/partnering-with-parents)
- *Children in the Worship Service* by David and Sally Michael
- *Family Discipleship Series* booklets

OTHER RESOURCES

- *The Church in Earnest* (especially Chapter 5) by John Angell James (book is free online)

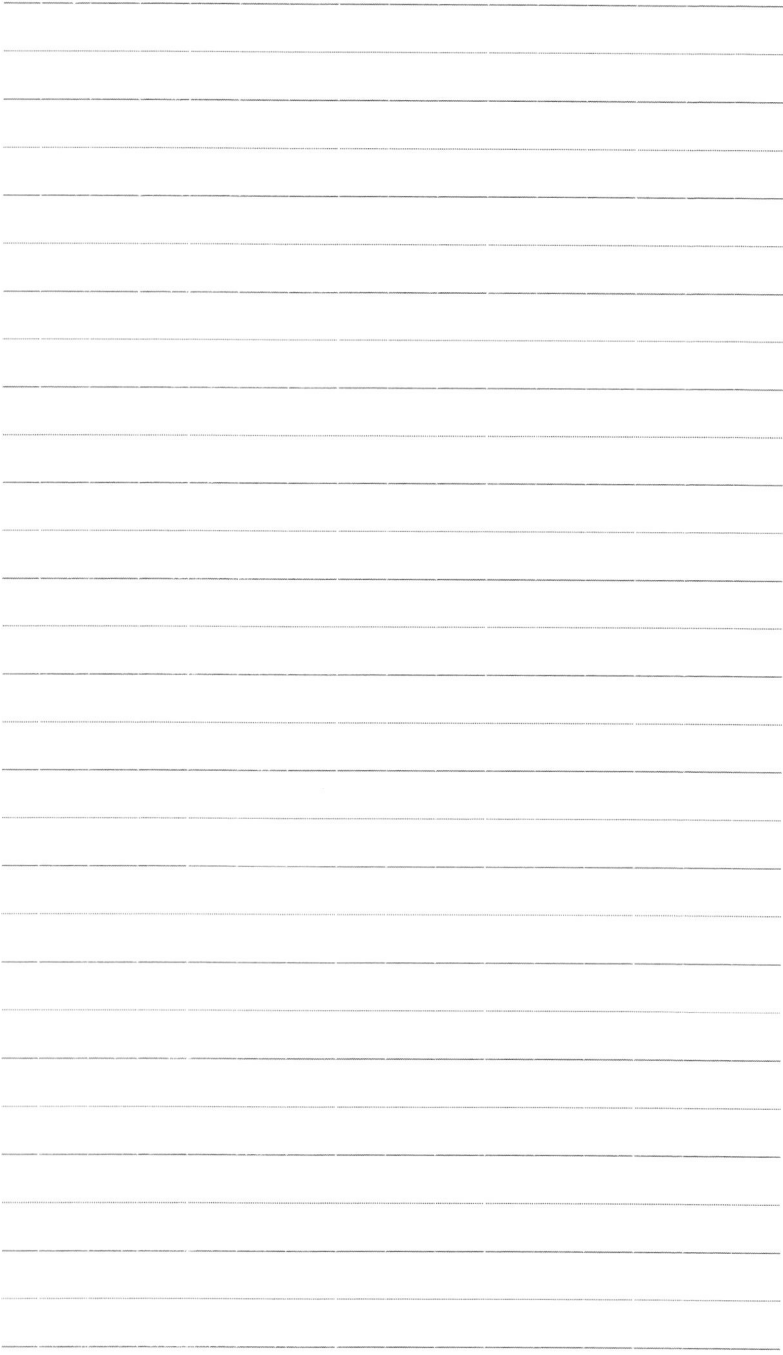

3

Teach the Breadth and Depth of the Whole Counsel of God

Often, young children are repeatedly told the same stories, while vast portions of Scripture are overlooked... When we limit the Scripture children are exposed to, we also limit their view of God. God needs to be seen in the vast array of His multifaceted character... Only through exposure to a variety of stories and biblical passages can children understand the balance of God's character—that He is merciful, yet just; that God is high and lofty, and yet He dwells in intimate fellowship with His people. (Zealous, page 46)

KEY SCRIPTURES

By the Holy Spirit who dwells within us, guard the good deposit entrusted to you... All Scripture is breathed out by God and profitable for teaching, for reproof, for correction, and for training in righteousness, that the man of God may be complete, equipped for every good work. (2 Timothy 1:14; 3:16-17)

Therefore I testify to you this day that I am innocent of the blood of all, for I did not shrink from declaring to you the whole counsel of God. (Acts 20:26-27)

"...I have made you a watchman for the house of Israel. Whenever you hear a word from my mouth, you shall give them warning from me... But if the watchman sees the sword coming and does not blow the trumpet, so that the people are not warned, and the sword comes and takes any one of them, that person is taken away in his iniquity, but his blood I will require at the watchman's hand." (Ezekiel 3:17, 33:6)

REFLECTION

It's possible to have zeal, biblical vision, and partnership with the church and home but still be lacking in the content and scope of what we are teaching. God's revealed Word is vast and profound, and the more we are exposed to the whole counsel of Scripture, the more we understand who God is, who we are, and how we should respond and live. We are all, by God's grace, growing in our understanding of the Bible, and discipleship is the fruit of our study, meditation, and application. By intentionally and comprehensively teaching the breadth and depth of the Bible, our children will have the essential knowledge needed for trusting and treasuring Christ and living as faithful disciples for God's glory.

Reflect on your exposure to the Bible when you were growing up and as an adult. How would you describe your grasp of the whole counsel of God's Word? Are there steps you can take to grow in your understanding of the breadth and depth of the Scriptures? Are there opportunities you can pursue to be more equipped to declare "the whole counsel of God" (Acts 20:27) to the children growing up in your church or home? Ask God for insights.

DISCUSSION

1. Give some examples of Bible stories that are repeated over and over to children. What are some other important stories and truths that are often overlooked? How might these overlooked stories and truths enhance your discipleship efforts?

2. Consider the implications of Acts 20:26-27 for parents, teachers, ministry leaders, and children. To what extent are you imparting the whole counsel of God in your church or home through the scope and sequence of what you teach to the next generation?

3. Consider Ezekiel 3:17 and 33:6. How is our responsibility (and accountability) as parents and ministry leaders similar to the "watchman on a wall"?

4. How would you explain the "breadth" and "depth" of God's Word? Why is it important for our children to be exposed to both?

On a scale of 1-10, rate how well your teaching includes both "breadth" and "depth" overall.

Little Breadth 1 2 3 4 5 6 7 8 9 10 Excellent Breadth

Little Depth 1 2 3 4 5 6 7 8 9 10 Excellent Depth

What is one thing that you or your ministry team could commit to that would grow these numbers?

_____

_____

NEXT STEPS

Ministry leaders—Incorporate Commitment #3 into your plan.

With the five categories on pages 49-50 of *Zealous* in mind, evaluate the materials used for the discipleship of the next generation growing up in your church or home (curriculum, books, resources for family devotions, vacation Bible school, camps, retreats, etc.):

- Bible survey and book studies
- Biblical theology
- Systematic theology
- Gospel proclamation
- Moral and ethical instruction

Are there any gaps? How might you come up with a plan to fill the gaps?

Are there Bible reading plans, Scripture memory tools, and catechism resources that can be used by or recommended to parents?

Parents—If you don't already have one, consider a plan for reading the Bible individually and as a family. Evaluate the devotional and other resources you use. Do they help your family grow in understanding the breadth and depth of God's Word? Consider including Scripture memory and catechism in your plan.

TRUTH78 RESOURCES

- Sunday School, Midweek, Multi-Age, and Backyard Bible Club/Vacation Bible School curricula (Truth78.org/curriculum-introduction)

- An explanation of Truth78's scope and sequence (Truth78.org/scope-sequence-explanation)
- *Growing in the Word* series
- *More Than a Story: Old Testament* and *More Than a Story: New Testament* by Sally Michael
- *Making HIM Known* devotional books
- Fighter Verses (fighterverses.com)

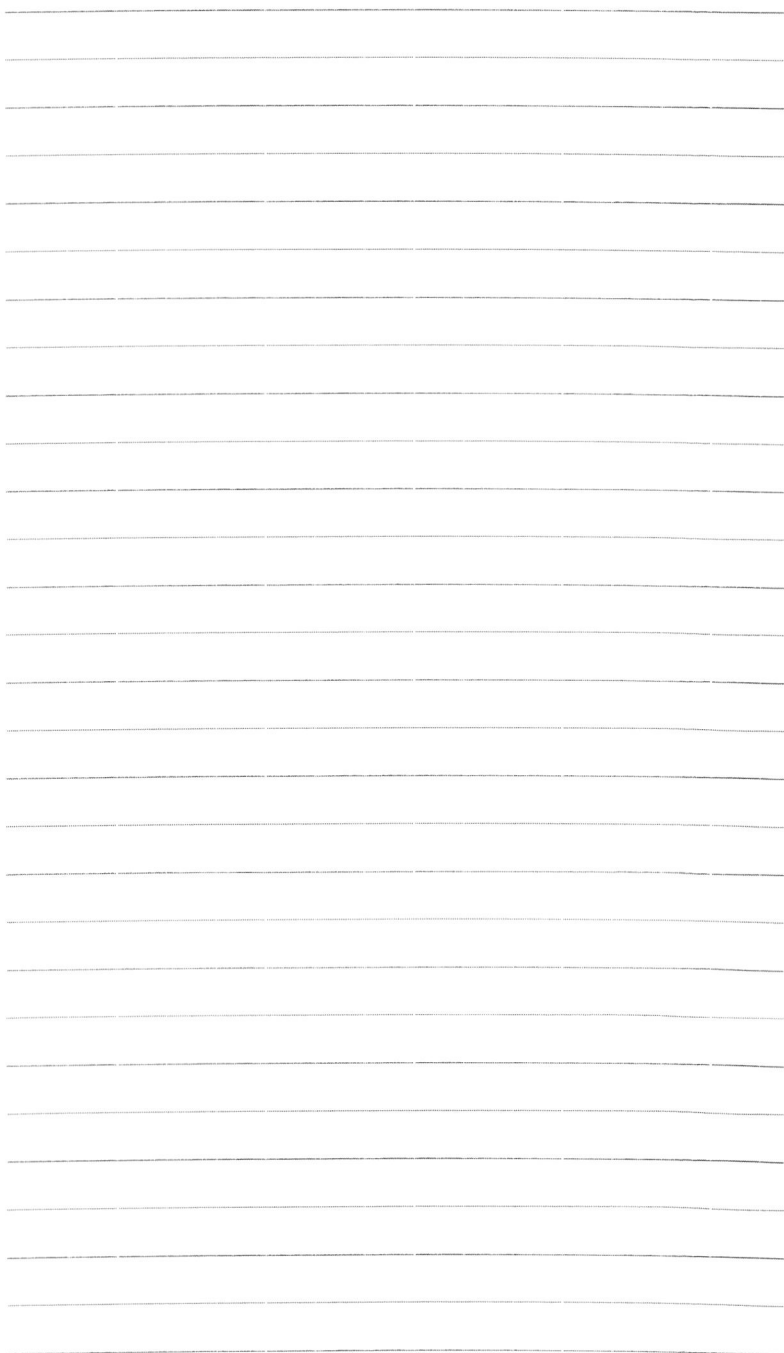

4

Proclaim the Glorious Gospel of Jesus Christ

As effective as we are in helping our children understand and believe the whole message of the gospel in all of its fullness and depth, we mustn't forget that the application of the gospel to the souls of our children takes a miracle that we cannot perform.... Yet, our efforts are often the very means by which God in His providence accomplishes His saving work. As we faithfully proclaim the glorious gospel of Jesus Christ, we labor with all our hearts, prayerfully and consistently guiding, inspiring, and exhorting the next generations toward a personal and sincere response to the gospel that bears the fruit of love, trust, and delight in God through Jesus Christ. (Zealous, pages 59-60)

KEY SCRIPTURES

*so that they should set their hope in God
and not forget the works of God,
but keep his commandments; (Psalm 78:7)*

*..."If anyone would come after me, let him deny himself and
take up his cross daily and follow me... What is impossible
with man is possible with God." (Luke 9:23; 18:27)*

*"...I will give them one heart, and a new spirit I will put
within them. I will remove the heart of stone from their
flesh and give them a heart of flesh," (Ezekiel 11:19)*

*"No one can come to me unless the Father who
sent me draws him..." (John 6:44a)*

REFLECTION

Ultimately, what drives our zeal, biblical vision, and discipleship strategies is our earnest desire for our children to trust and treasure Jesus Christ alone for the forgiveness of their sins and the fulfillment of all His promises to them, including eternal life. It is often difficult to discern genuine faith in children (or anyone, for that matter). While we affirm that salvation is by grace alone through faith alone in Christ alone, there are foundational truths throughout the Old and New Testaments that help us guide our children to a sincere and genuine response to the gospel. The call to raise a generation that hopes in God requires that we, as ministry leaders and parents, tell all of God's glorious deeds, especially His glorious plan for the salvation of His people. Praise God for His sovereign grace and transforming power to raise hearts that are dead in sin to new life in Christ!

Consider ways you can deepen your own understanding and appreciation of the essential truths of the gospel. How can you help the next generation within your sphere of influence grow in their understanding and appreciation of these truths?

DISCUSSION

1. Based on what you observed of the interaction between Ethan and Mr. Johnson (*Zealous*, pages 53-55), what raises confidence or concern about the genuineness of Ethan's faith?

2. Think about a child in your household or church who professes faith in Christ. What gives you confidence or concern about the genuineness of his/her faith?

3. Are there young people you know who are trusting Christ and seem to grasp the breadth and depth of the gospel? How did they come to this understanding? What implications does this have for the discipleship of the next generation in your church or household?

4. Discuss the concern about "an overemphasis on explicitly linking every Bible lesson to Jesus and the gospel," especially when teaching the Old Testament (page 57). Is this a valid concern?

5. What are some ideas you have for integrating the "10 Essential Gospel Truths" into your teaching or discipleship opportunities?

_____

_____

_____

_____

On a scale of 1-10, rate how well the "10 Essential Gospel Truths" are included in what you teach overall.

Not Included 1 2 3 4 5 6 7 8 9 10 Fully Included

What is one thing that you or your ministry team could commit to that would grow this number?

_____

_____

NEXT STEPS

Ministry leaders—Incorporate Commitment #4 into your plan.

Take time to reflect on each of the "10 Essential Gospel Truths" and the corresponding Scripture references on pages 119-121 of *Zealous*. Include them in your strategic plan and consider specific ways you might use them to train and equip staff, teachers, and volunteers.

- Does your next-generation ministry plan include gospel proclamation that has both breadth and depth versus a more simplistic approach?

- Are there steps you can take in baptism and membership preparation to better discern a young person's understanding of the gospel and the genuineness of his/her faith?

- Is there a way that you can involve parents in this preparation process?

Parents—Memorize the "10 Essential Gospel Truths" and develop a plan to regularly rehearse these truths—individually with your child or as a family study.

TRUTH78 RESOURCES

- *Helping Children to Understand the Gospel* by Sally Michael, Jill Nelson, and Bud Burk
- *God's Gospel* by Jill Nelson
- *Established in the Faith* by David Michael
- *Glorious God, Glorious Gospel* by Sally Michael and Jill Nelson
- *The World Created, Fallen, Redeemed, and Restored* by Sally Michael
- *The Greatest Treasure!* by Jill Nelson
- *The Greatest Gift!* by Jill Nelson

OTHER RESOURCES

- *What is the Gospel?* by Greg Gilbert
- *Your Child's Profession of Faith* by Dennis Gundersen
- *The Faith of a Child: A Step-by-Step Guide to Salvation for Your Child* by Art Murphy

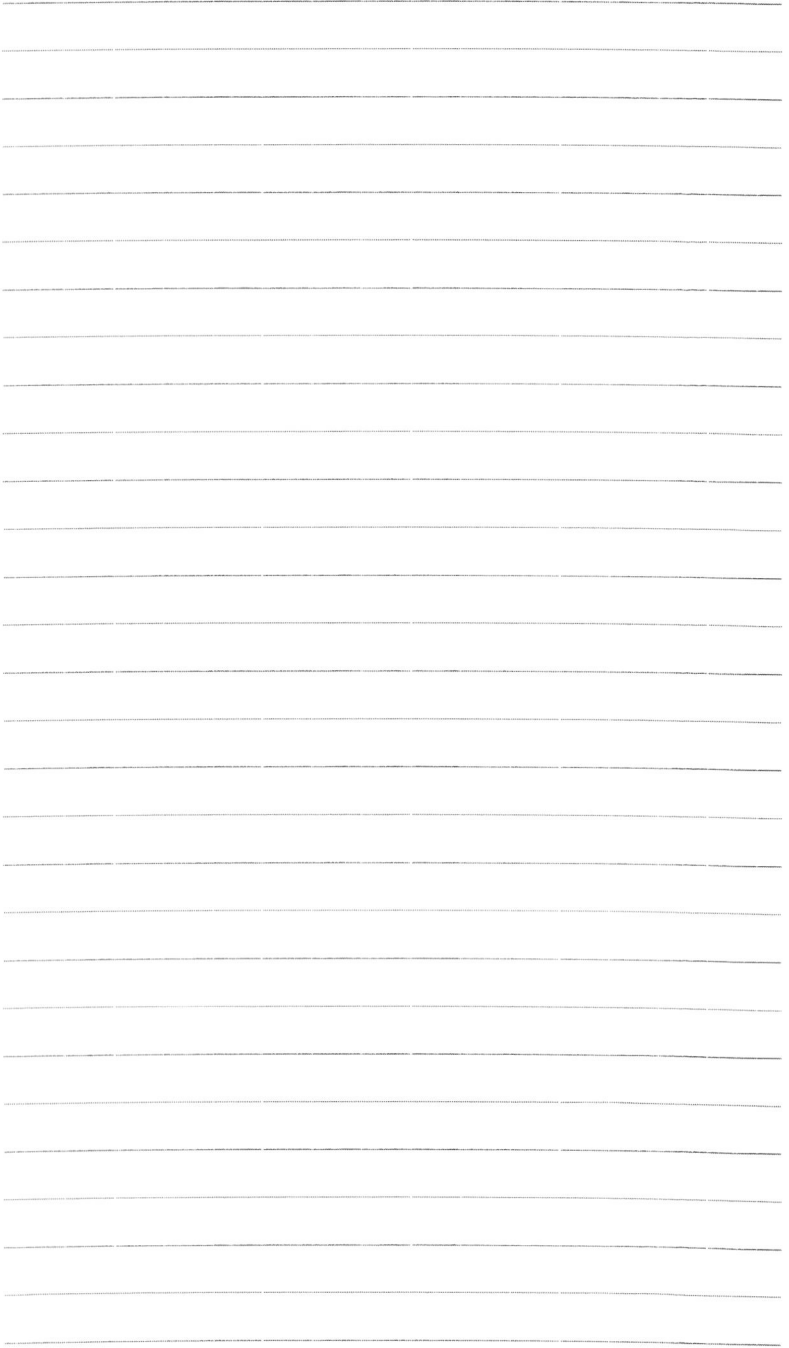

Disciple the Mind, Heart, and Will

*It's not enough for children just to know what the Bible says and
teaches. Crucial for the fruitful discipleship of the next generation is
the opportunity to instruct the mind, engage the heart, and influence
the will... Though we do not always see the result of our teaching—the
informing of the mind with truth—we must help children understand
how to apply the truth to their own lives. If they own that truth,
embracing it in their hearts, the Holy Spirit will bring opportunities
to act on the truth, engaging the will. (Zealous, pages 61-62)*

KEY SCRIPTURES

*Do your best to present yourself to God as one approved,
a worker who has no need to be ashamed, rightly
handling the word of truth. (2 Timothy 2:15)*

*"This people honors me with their lips,
but their heart is far from me;" (Matthew 15:8)*

*I delight to do your will, O my God;
your law is within my heart. (Psalm 40:8)*

*"Everyone then who hears these words of mine and does them will
be like a wise man who built his house on the rock. And the rain fell,
and the floods came, and the winds blew and beat on that house,
but it did not fall, because it had been founded on the rock. And
everyone who hears these words of mine and does not do them will
be like a foolish man who built his house on the sand. And the rain
fell, and the floods came, and the winds blew and beat against that
house, and it fell, and great was the fall of it." (Matthew 7:24-27)*

REFLECTION

Opportunities abound for teaching God's Word and sharing the gospel in our homes and churches. However, we recognize that knowledge alone is not saving faith—and neither emotional experiences, behavior modification, nor godly living alone prove a genuinely transformed heart. We were not created as one-dimensional beings, and neither were our children. That's why it's important to reach the mind, heart, and will when discipling the next generation. Biblical vision, partnership between the church and home, and resources that teach the depth and breadth of the Bible and proclaim the essential truths of the gospel help us do just that. (Are you noticing how all the commitments work together for the discipleship of the next generation?) Ultimately, we trust God to use our efforts to open the eyes of our children, rescue them from their sin, and give them the power to walk in the newness of life. But we have the privilege of modeling and imparting "the glorious deeds of the LORD" (Psalm 78:4) in multi-dimensional ways—in the hope that children and youth will, by God's grace, come to know, embrace, and apply biblical truth. We want our children to love God and walk in His ways!

In what ways are you integrating all three dimensions of discipleship (mind, heart, and will) into your efforts? Ask God to show you tangible ways to model and impart biblical truth where there are weaknesses or gaps.

DISCUSSION

1. Discuss the Psalm 32 example of Sally on pages 61-62 of *Zealous*. Have you had similar experiences in the classroom or with a child at home? Share stories of God at work during moments like this.

2. What opportunities are children in your church or home given to interact with a physical copy of the Bible? Would you agree that "hands-on active learning" (page 64) has the potential to hinder biblical instruction of the mind?

3. Which of the four ways to engage the heart on pages 66-67 have you found to be the most effective in your teaching? What new ideas for engaging the heart would you like to try?

4. Which of the six ways for influencing the will on pages 68-69 have you found effective? What new ideas for influencing the will would you like to try?

5. What are some ways parents or teachers can illustrate through their example what it means to know, embrace, and apply biblical truth?

_____

_____

_____

_____

On a scale of 1-10, rate how well you "instruct the mind, engage the heart, and influence the will" overall.

Not Well 1 2 3 4 5 6 7 8 9 10 Extremely Well

What is one thing that you or your ministry team could commit to that would grow this number?

_____

_____

NEXT STEPS

Ministry leaders—Incorporate Commitment #5 into your plan.

Discuss the ideas in this chapter for modeling and implementing a multi-dimensional approach to discipleship. Consider other ideas you or your group may have for intentionally discipling the mind, heart, and will. As you reflect on what you've developed in your ministry plan so far, consider how you will implement the ideas and encourage parents and teachers as they impart biblical truth and find ways to help children and youth apply it to their lives.

Parents—As your children learn biblical truth at church or you teach them at home, build on the discipleship of the mind with the ideas on pages 66-69 of *Zealous* to reinforce the knowledge to disciple their hearts and wills.

TRUTH78 RESOURCES

- An explanation of the Truth78 scope and sequence (Truth78.org/scope-sequence-explanation)
- *Discipleship Through Doctrinal Teaching & Catechism* by Sally Michael
- *Mothers: Disciplers of the Next Generations* by Sally Michael

OTHER RECOMMENDED RESOURCES FOR CHRISTIAN EDUCATION DIRECTORS

- *Teaching to Change Lives: Seven Proven Ways to Make Your Teaching Come Alive* by Dr. Howard Hendricks
- *Creative Bible Teaching* by Lawrence O. Richards and Gary J. Bredfeldt

OTHER RECOMMENDED RESOURCES FOR PARENTS

- *Gospel-Powered Parenting: How the Gospel Shapes and Transforms Parenting* by William P. Farley
- *The Disciple-Making Parent: A Comprehensive Guidebook for Raising Your Children to Love and Follow Jesus Christ* by Chap Bettis
- *Teach Them Diligently: How to Use the Scriptures in Child Training* by Lou Priolo
- *Shepherding a Child's Heart* by Tedd Tripp
- *Instructing a Child's Heart* by Tedd and Margy Tripp
- *Age of Opportunity: A Biblical Guide to Parenting Teens* by Paul Tripp
- *Reaching Your Child's Heart: A Practical Guide to Faithful Parenting* by Juan and Jeanine Sanchez
- *Parenting Essentials: Equipping Your Children for Life* by Andreas and Margaret Köstenberger

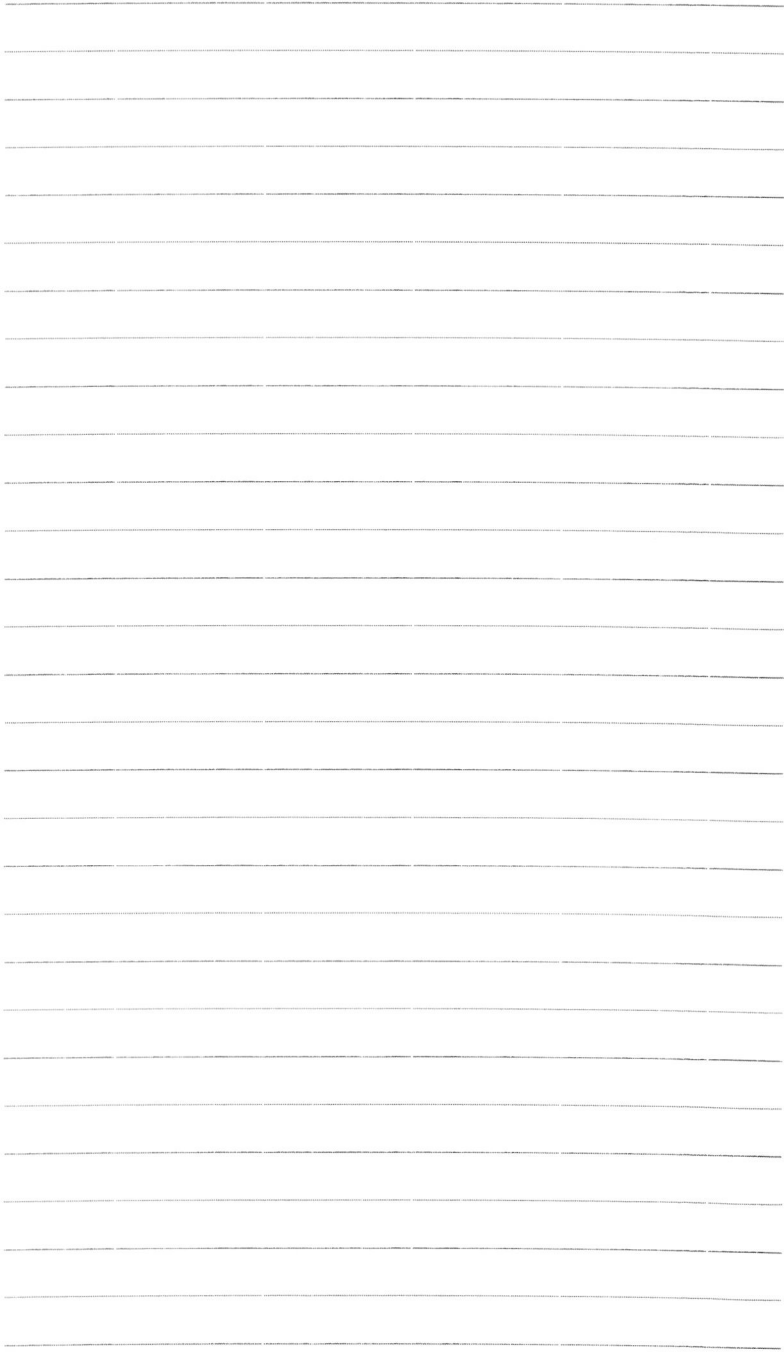

6

Pray with Dependence on God's Sovereign Grace

The most important thing I can do to provide what I desire for my children is to seek God's help and plead for His grace to accomplish what I am powerless to do in the heart of my child... That's why being seriously committed to the discipleship of the next generation means being seriously committed to praying regularly, earnestly, and biblically for the faith of the next generation. God's power in the gospel of Jesus Christ, His unstoppable purposes for our children, and our inescapable responsibility to raise them in the faith all come together in prayer. (Zealous, page 74)

KEY SCRIPTURES

For by grace you have been saved through faith. And this is not your own doing; it is the gift of God, not a result of works, so that no one may boast. (Ephesians 2:8-9)

..."Satan demanded to have you, that he might sift you like wheat, but I have prayed for you that your faith may not fail..." (Luke 22:31-32a)

"The LORD bless you and keep you; the LORD make his face to shine upon you and be gracious to you; the LORD lift up his countenance upon you and give you peace." (Numbers 6:24-26)

REFLECTION

All our actionable efforts to cast vision, partner together, teach, proclaim, instruct, engage, and influence for the faith of the next generation accomplish nothing apart from God's providential help. We are dependent on His redeeming work in the hearts and lives of our children—and He is faithfully at work in a million ways! Opportunities abound at church and home to pursue God individually and corporately in prayer for the deep desires we have for our children and the fulfillment of His purposes for their lives. Establishing a habit of praying "big, bold, biblical prayers"[1] can accomplish more than we imagine for the faith of our children and will continue to bear fruit for generations to come.

How would you describe your rhythm of prayer for your children? When you pray for your children, what do you pray for? What steps can you take to grow in the discipline of prayer, especially for the next generation growing up in your church and family? Take time to pray for your children and the children in your church.

---

1 *Big, Bold, Biblical Prayers for the Next Generation* by David Michael, available through Truth78.org

DISCUSSION

1. What from this chapter most encouraged, challenged, motivated, or convicted you?

2. In what ways does next-generation ministry in your church or home reflect the priority of prayer? What more can you do to encourage or prioritize prayer?

3. What are some key passages of Scripture that can inform and shape your prayers for the next generation?

4. Using some of the passages, take some extended time individually, with a spouse or friend, and/or as a group to pray for the next generation within your sphere of influence and for any specific requests.

On a scale of 1-10, rate how consistently (or regularly) you are praying with dependence on God for the next generation overall.

Not Consistent 1 2 3 4 5 6 7 8 9 10 Extremely Consistent

What is one thing that you or your ministry team could commit to that would grow this number?

_____

_____

NEXT STEPS

Ministry leaders—Incorporate Commitment #6 into your plan.

Look for ways to inspire and equip parents, teachers, children's and youth workers, church leaders, and the congregation as a whole. Perhaps share some of the suggested prayers on pages 78-79 of *Zealous* to help prompt people to pray that...

- the Holy Spirit would be present, bringing a spirit of peace and order to our classroom.
- God would be at work causing the children to have attentive ears, minds, and hearts.
- all our attitudes, words, and actions would serve to glorify God, edify the children, and point them to the incomparable treasure of Jesus.
- God would protect us and the children from unhelpful distractions and the darts of the enemy.
- God's Word would be clearly proclaimed by the teachers and understood by the children.
- visitors would feel loved and welcomed.
- children with special needs would be loved, served, and included.
- children would extend grace, patience, and love to one another.
- gospel truths would be embraced with genuine faith.
- our worship time would be filled with expressions of true love and praise.
- small group leaders would be given wisdom and discernment as they seek to lead the children to respond to the truths presented.
- we would respond in wise and God-honoring ways to rebellious hearts, inattentiveness, inappropriate silliness, etc.

- parents would feel assisted and helped, and would be moved and equipped to actively disciple their children in the home.
- every child in our classroom would, by God's sovereign grace, grow and mature into a man or woman wholly devoted to Jesus Christ.

Consider organizing a special prayer event or regular meeting specifically for parents.

Ministry leaders and parents—What steps can you take to increase prayer for the next generation in your church or family? Here are some examples:

- Match every child in the church with a prayer partner from the congregation who commits to pray regularly for him or her.
- Encourage teachers and small group leaders to pray weekly for every child or youth in their class or group and their parents by name.
- Form prayer teams to pray for children, nursery workers, teachers, and other volunteers during the Sunday school hour.
- Taking inspiration from George McCluskey (pages 75-76), set aside one meal, one day a week, to pray and fast for the next generation.
- Provide every father and grandfather with a copy of *A Father's Guide to Blessing His Children.*

TRUTH78 RESOURCES

- *Big, Bold, Biblical Prayers for the Next Generation* by David Michael
- *Praying for the Next Generation* by Sally Michael
- *A Father's Guide to Blessing His Children* by David Michael
- *Utter Dependency on God, Through Prayer* by Bud Burk

OTHER RESOURCES

- *A Praying Life: Connecting with God in a Distracting World* by Paul E. Miller

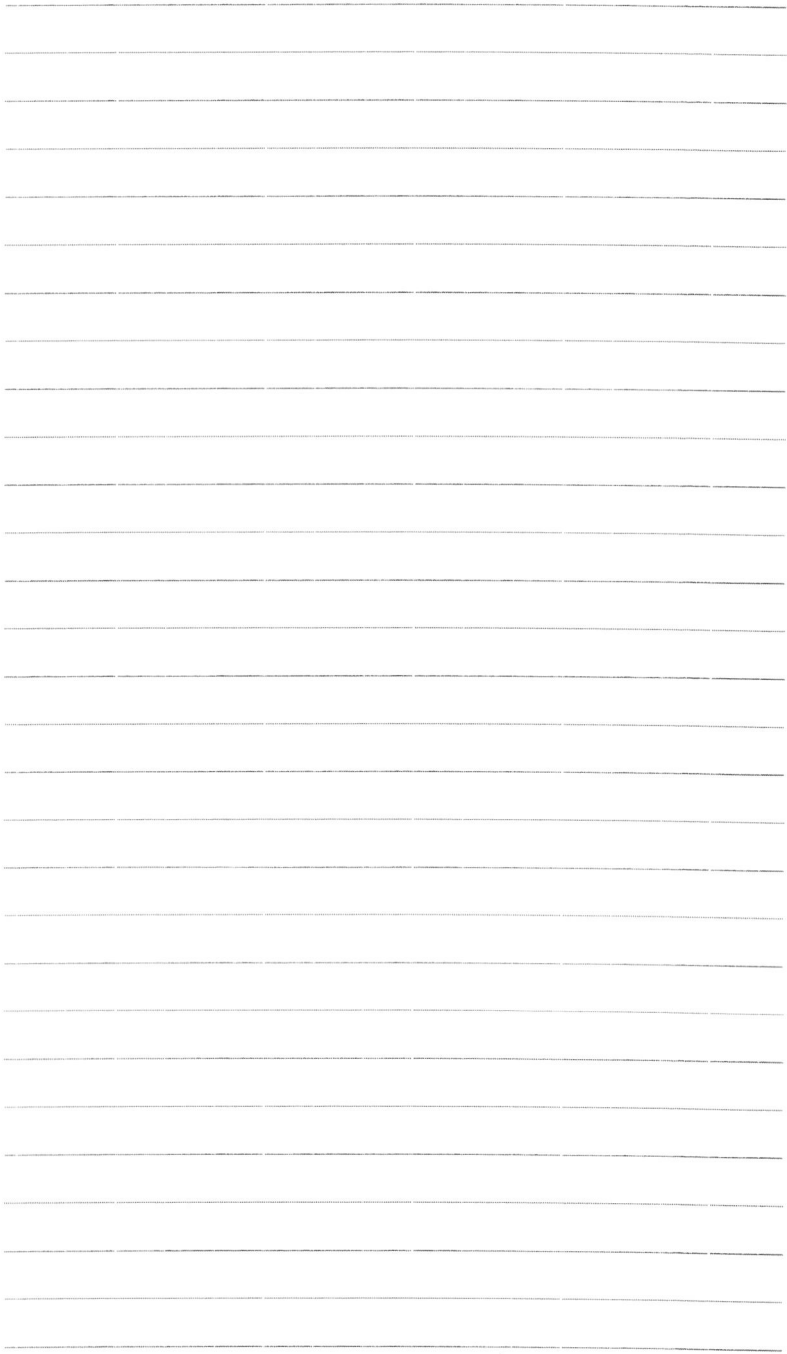

7

Inspire Worship of God, for the Glory of God

When we emphasize God's glory by declaring His glorious deeds, we are providing the God-ordained fuel for worship. Nothing in me wants to sing when you tell me how special Shadrach, Meshach, and Abednego were. But when you show me a God who rules over the forces of nature and defeats the forces of wickedness to accomplish His unstoppable purposes for His glory and the joy of His people, "then sings my soul" to the praise of God's glory and grace. (Zealous, page 90)

KEY SCRIPTURES

So, whether you eat or drink, or whatever you do, do all to the glory of God. (1 Corinthians 10:31)

*..."bring my sons from afar
and my daughters from the end of the earth,
everyone who is called by my name,
whom I created for my glory,
whom I formed and made." (Isaiah 43:6b-7)*

*Great is the LORD, and greatly to be praised,
and his greatness is unsearchable.
One generation shall commend your works to another,
and shall declare your mighty acts. (Psalm 145:3-4)*

REFLECTION

The 7 Commitments culminate with the ultimate goal of the discipleship of the next generation and the object of our zeal—the glory of God! Throughout the Bible, we see God's desire to make His glory known to generation after generation. We've reflected on many passages, like Psalm 78, that point to our role to "tell the coming generation the glorious deeds of the LORD…" (verse 4). We've also considered a theological framework and practical ideas for carrying out this call faithfully, comprehensively, and collectively. All of this is to inspire our children to worship our glorious God in the splendor of His holiness with reverence and awe for His glory. The aim of our discipleship efforts is to magnify the glory of the Triune God for the soul-satisfying, everlasting joy of the next generation. So together we sing:

Praise God, from whom all blessings flow.
Praise Him, all creatures here below.
Praise Him, above, ye heavenly hosts.
Praise Father, Son, and Holy Ghost.

Even now, let's take some time to worship and magnify our great God as He reveals Himself in His Word. Write down any thoughts you have for inspiring the next generation to worship and glorify God. Ask God to open the eyes of your heart to see wonderful things in His Word.

DISCUSSION

1. Discuss the implications of Psalm 78:4 on pages 87-88 of *Zealous*. In what ways may God's glorious deeds be hidden from the children growing up in your church or family?

2. What are some ways that you can more effectively magnify the glory in God's "glorious deeds" when instructing the next generation in your church and home?

3. What are some specific ways that parents, teachers, and others in your church can be equipped to distinguish the difference between God-centered and man-centered worship?

4. What are some practical ways to encourage children to respond with worship to the truths they are learning at church and at home?

NEXT STEPS

Ministry leaders—Incorporate Commitment #7 into your plan.

Consider the following:

- What, if any, steps do you need to take to keep from hiding the glory of God from the next generation and ensure that the instruction they receive, the songs they sing, and the activities they do reinforce a God-centered perspective?

- If children are not encouraged to participate in the corporate worship gathering in your church, read *Children and the Worship Service* by David and Sally Michael, and consider ways to encourage families to attend together.

- Consider hosting a prayer and praise night for families. Include Scripture, the attributes of God, the names of God, hymns and songs, and prayers of adoration.

Parents—If you don't already have time set aside for family worship, make it your goal to establish a habit of meeting together, reading the Bible, and praising God for His greatness and worth. Help your children respond with worship to the truths they learn from your instruction. Memorizing hymns and portions of Scripture (e.g., the psalms) can be a helpful way to give children a vocabulary for praise and adoration of God. Also, in the spirit of Deuteronomy 6:7, don't miss the opportunities God gives you every day for spontaneous worship "when you sit in your house, and when you walk by the way, and when you lie down, and when you rise."

TRUTH78 RESOURCES

- *A Vision for God-Centered, Gospel-Focused Teaching for the Next Generations*, video by David and Sally Michael sharing the foundations of a God-centered children's ministry (Truth78.org/foundations-for-ministry)

OTHER RESOURCES

- *Family Worship: In the Bible, In History, and In Your Home* by Donald S. Whitney
- *Family Worship* by Joel R. Beeke
- Resources from Getty Music

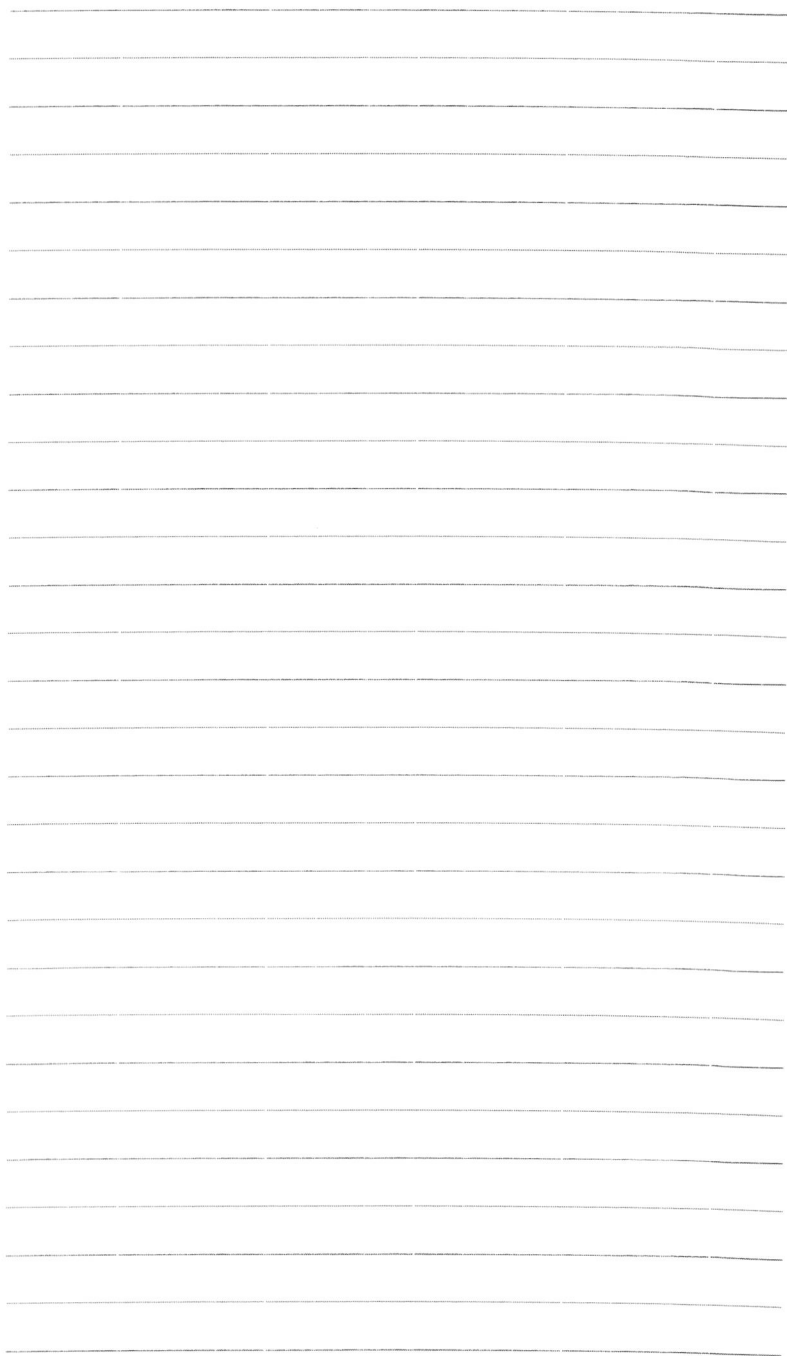

Persevering in Zeal

God forbid that any of us would lose heart for the ministry of the gospel that we have received by the mercy of God. The very thought should make us tremble. We cannot lose heart in reflecting the knowledge of the glory of God. We must not lose heart in displaying the surpassing power of Christ—to the world—or to those who are being transformed from one degree of glory to another. To throw in the towel on the gospel is to believe in vain... Belief is characterized by holding fast with zeal. (Zealous, pages 94-95)

KEY SCRIPTURES

Therefore, having this ministry by the mercy of God, we do not lose heart... For this light momentary affliction is preparing for us an eternal weight of glory beyond all comparison, as we look not to the things that are seen but to the things that are unseen. For the things that are seen are transient, but the things that are unseen are eternal. (2 Corinthians 4:1,17-18)

Now to him who is able to do far more abundantly than all that we ask or think, according to the power at work within us, to him be glory in the church and in Christ Jesus throughout all generations, forever and ever. Amen. (Ephesians 3:20-21)

..."My grace is sufficient for you, for my power is made perfect in weakness." Therefore I will boast all the more gladly of my weaknesses, so that the power of Christ may rest upon me. For the sake of Christ, then, I am content with weaknesses, insults, hardships, persecutions, and calamities. For when I am weak, then I am strong. (2 Corinthians 12:9-10)

REFLECTION

Please don't give up! Don't lose heart and shrink back or settle for mediocrity when the task of discipleship seems overwhelming, circumstances seem impossible to overcome, and temptations abound. Take heart! Our God is a mighty God! He magnifies His strength in our weakness. He can multiply the loaves and fishes of our efforts and feed thousands. He always finishes what He starts. We can press on in hope, confident that God is able to exceed our prayers and accomplish abundantly beyond all we ask or think—for His glory, and for the everlasting joy and good of the next generation. Let's keep growing in these commitments, trusting that God is faithful!

Think about your journey through *Zealous* and all that you have gleaned from considering God's Word, responding to what you have read, reflecting on concepts, tackling questions with others, and applying ideas to your church and family. In what ways have you been impacted by this study? Ask God for more grace to pursue zeal for the discipleship of the next generation.

DISCUSSION

1. Have you been tempted in the past, or are you maybe even being tempted now to lose heart as a parent or ministry leader? Describe your experience.

2. What are some of the small or big mercies of God that have helped you persevere in your discipleship efforts? How have you found God's grace to be sufficient in challenging times?

3. What ideas do you have to help each other focus on what is "unseen" and "keep eternity in view" as parents or a ministry team?

On a scale of 1-10, rate how hopeful and encouraged you are in your ministry overall.

Ready To Quit 1   2   3   4   5   6   7   8   9   10 Full Of Encouragement

What is one thing that you or your ministry team could commit to that would grow this number?

NEXT STEPS

Ministry leaders—Finalize your strategic plan.

Think about a strategy for helping yourself or others persevere in faithful discipleship for the sake of the next generations. Do you have people in your life who can remind you of what is true and encourage you to not lose heart? Is there a resource, conference, or training that could be helpful for you as you seek to maintain an eternal perspective?

How can you encourage parents to press on in their discipleship efforts? What support is available for couples and families?

Put the finishing touches on your strategic plan, adding anything unique to the culture or rhythm of your church congregation. If you haven't already done so, consider getting feedback from other leaders, teachers, and parents.

Parents—Seek the support of your church, a mentor couple, a small group, etc. for encouragement to persevere as you face the various seasons and challenges of parenting.

Press on!

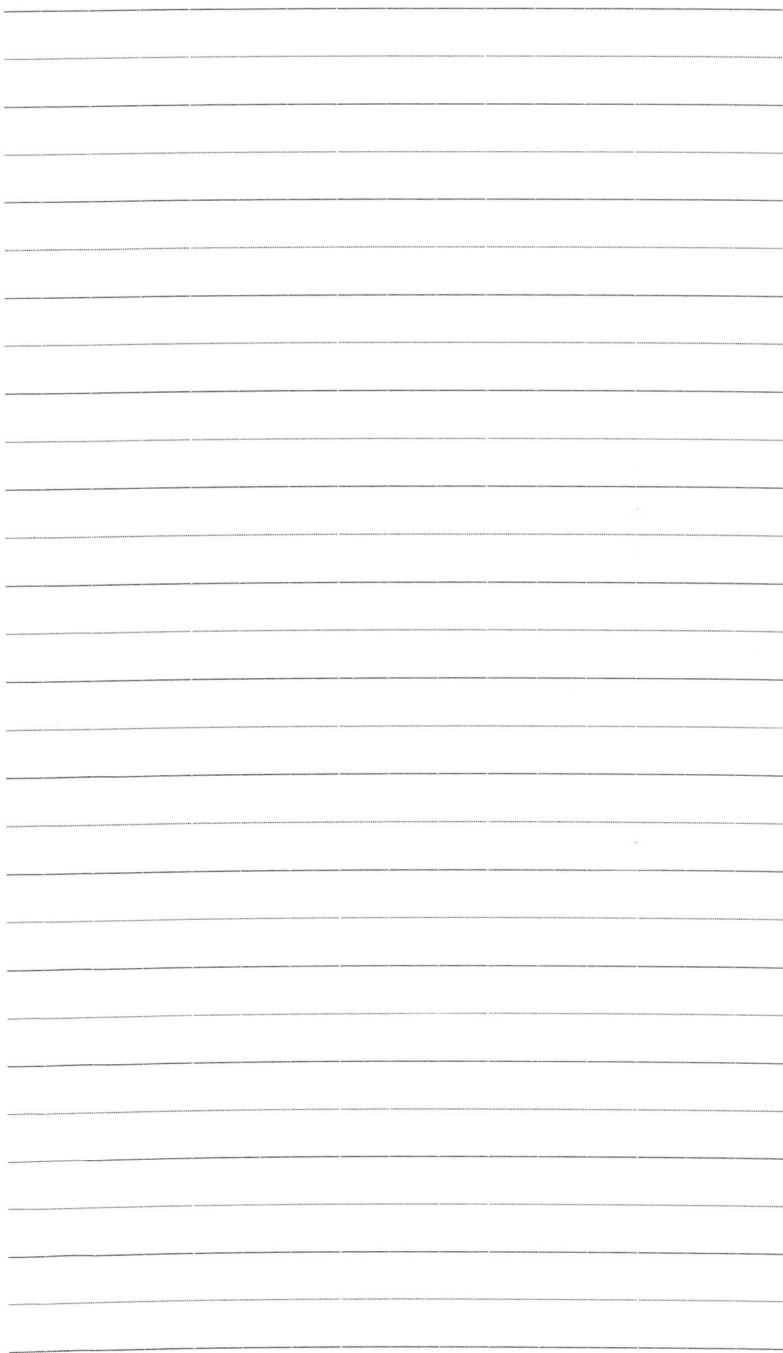

Truth78

Our vision is that the next generations may know, honor, and treasure God, setting their hope in Christ alone, so that they will live as faithful disciples for the glory of God.

It is our mission to inspire and equip the church and home for the comprehensive discipleship of the next generation. To that end, we develop resources that put God at the center, focus on the gospel, and exalt Christ. They are grounded in sound doctrine for faithful discipleship.

RESOURCES AND TRAINING MATERIALS

CURRICULUM

We publish materials for formal Bible instruction in the classroom including Sunday School, Midweek programs, Backyard Bible Clubs/VBS, and multi-age studies. The scope and sequence reflects our commitment to teach children and youth the whole counsel of God over the course of their education. Most materials can easily be adapted for use in Christian schools and homeschools.

VISION-CASTING AND TRAINING

We offer a wide variety of booklets, video and audio seminars, articles, and other practical training resources designed to assist ministry leaders, volunteers, and parents to implement Truth78's vision and mission in their churches and homes. Many are available for free at Truth78.org.

PARENTING AND FAMILY DISCIPLESHIP

Truth78 equips parents to disciple their children with booklets, video presentations, family devotionals, children's books, articles, apps, and more. Curricula include take-home pages to help parents nurture faith at home by applying classroom lessons to their child's daily experience.

BIBLE MEMORY

Truth78 publishes Fighter Verses, the collection of 260 passages uniquely suited to arm individuals, families, and whole churches for the fight of faith.

Companion resources include study guides, journals, coloring books, and songs to encourage Scripture memory, as well as Foundation Verses to help toddlers and preschoolers lay a firm biblical foundation.

For more information about resources and services, please contact us.

Truth78.org ◆ info@Truth78.org ◆ (877) 400-1414